The GREAT OUTDOORS

GARDEN

LISA REGAN

WAYLAND
www.waylandbooks.co.uk

First published in Great Britain in 2019
by Wayland
Copyright © Hodder and Stoughton, 2019
All rights reserved

Created for Wayland by www.squareandcircus.co.uk
Illustrations: Supriya Sahai
Editor: John Hort

HB ISBN: 978 1 5263 1103 0
PB ISBN: 978 1 5263 1104 7

Printed and bound in China

Wayland, an imprint of
Hachette Children's Group
Part of Hodder and Stoughton
Carmelite House
50 Victoria Embankment
London EC4Y 0DZ
An Hachette UK Company
www.hachette.co.uk
www.hachettechildrens.co.uk

MIX
Paper from
responsible sources
FSC® C104740
FSC
www.fsc.org

Picture credits: All images Shutterstock: Africa Studio 4a;
PhotoFires 5a; Inspired Vision Studio 5b; 2009fotofriends 5c;
Del Boy 6a; Tom Karola 8a; Dewin' Indew 8b; Jirasak
Chuangsen 9a; Sommai 10a; peterfactors 11a; Marija Stepanovic
11b; Alena Brozova 11c; Alison Hancock 12a; P Maxwell
Photography13a; Franz Peter Rudolf 14a; DioGen 16a; Ruth Swan
16b; Giedriius 16c; Sarah2 16d; D. Kucharski K. Kucharska 17a;
Marija Stepanovic 17b; Derren 17c; BushAlex 17d;
Ivan Smuk 17e; Prachaya Roekdeethaweesab 17f; Suchatbky
17g; Jack Hong 17h; Luc Pouliot 17i; kevin whitehouse 18a;
taviphoto 18b; clarst5 18c; Mike Truchon 18d; D and
D Photo Sudbury 18e; El Coronesta 18f; serkan
mutan 19a; kojihirano 19b; Jak1Zdenek 19c;
Steve Byland 19d; Eric Isselee 19e; Dr Morley
Read 21a; Bildagentur Zoonar GmbH 22a, 22b,
23a, 23b; alison1414 24a; Gabor Havasi 27a;
Leigh Trail 28a; josefkubes 29a; Angurt 29b.
Cover: pixel creator.

Every attempt has been made to clear copyright.
Should there be any inadvertent omission please apply
to the publisher for rectification.

CONTENTS

WHAT IS A GARDEN?

A garden is an area, often next to a house, where people can grow plants. Some people like to create something colourful or grow their own food, while others choose plants that attract wildlife. Families also often design their garden as a place for children to play.

Under control

Common garden tasks include pruning and weeding. Plants are pruned, or cut back, to stop them growing too big. Weeds are plants that grow where they're not wanted. That might be a daisy in the middle of a lawn, or a wildflower in a rose bed. Some people plant wildflowers in their gardens on purpose, to attract insects.

Plants such as lilac have a strong sweet or spicy scent.

You can grow food in a tiny space.

Grass is hardwearing. Lots of running and jumping doesn't kill it.

Glorious gardens

Some gardens are particularly extravagant and special. Millions of people visit them every year. The gardens at the palace of Versailles in France were designed in the 1600s. They cover more land than 800 football pitches and are carefully laid out to make beautiful shapes.

The Yuyuan Garden in Shanghai, China, is planted with trees that burst into life in the spring. It has ponds, bridges, caves, sculptures and towers.

The Butchart Gardens in British Columbia are a National Historic Site of Canada, built in an old quarry.

PLANNING A GARDEN

A clever gardener chooses a variety of plants that grow to different heights and flower in different seasons. The plants are usually placed in different areas, depending on how much sun or shade they need, and the type of soil they thrive in.

Towering trees

Trees provide shade from the sunshine and shelter from wind and frost. They are home to wildlife such as birds and squirrels. Some give us food, such as fruit and nuts.

Climbing plants grow upwards and often take up very little ground space. Some need fastening to a wall or a fence, but others cling to structures themselves.

Woody plants that don't grow very tall are often called **shrubs** or bushes.

On the ground

Alpine plants grow well in sunny spots with poor soil. They often have small leaves and bright flowers. Their shallow roots spread across large areas to gather **nutrients**.

Alpine plants grow well in a **rock garden** or **rockery**.

Foxglove

Sweet pea

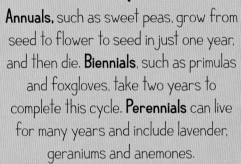
Lavender

Life cycle

Annuals, such as sweet peas, grow from seed to flower to seed in just one year, and then die. **Biennials**, such as primulas and foxgloves, take two years to complete this cycle. **Perennials** can live for many years and include lavender, geraniums and anemones.

DID YOU KNOW?

Perennials can be evergreen, which means they keep their stems and leaves through the winter, or deciduous, which means the part of the plant above the ground dies back in autumn or winter.

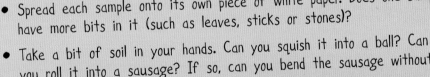
TRY THIS...

SOIL TESTING

There are three main types of soil: clay, silt and sand. Which is in your garden?

- Use a trowel to dig down about 10 cm to get a cupful of soil from three places in your garden. Compare the different colours and textures.

- Spread each sample onto its own piece of white paper. Does one sample have more bits in it (such as leaves, sticks or stones)?

- Take a bit of soil in your hands. Can you squish it into a ball? Can you roll it into a sausage? If so, can you bend the sausage without it breaking?

- Sandy soil feels gritty and does not stick together. Silt soil squishes together but crumbles again. Clay soil is easy to roll and bend and turns shiny if you rub it with your fingers.

- Which soil is in your garden? Is it the same soil throughout?

Digging in the dirt

Soil is full of **bacteria** that break down dead **organic matter**. This is good for soil, but can be harmful to humans, which is why you should <u>wear gardening gloves and wash your hands really well</u> after you have worked in the garden.

A small pond is home to fish and frogs, and attracts birds and dragonflies.

FLOWERING AND NON-FLOWERING PLANTS

Flowers fill a garden with colour and scent, although not all plants have flowers. A flower helps a plant to reproduce by attracting animals, including insects, but some plants reproduce in different ways.

New blooms

A flower contains both male and female parts (see page 9). The male parts hold pollen, which has to be moved to another flower and brought into contact with the female part. This **fertilises** the flower and allows it to make seeds, which can be carried far and wide and grow into new plants.

Flowers have scented or coloured petals to attract **pollinators** such as bees.

No blooms

Ferns and mosses do not produce flowers. Instead, they make **spores** that blow on the wind and grow into new plants where they land. Coniferous trees, such as firs and pines, have pollen and seeds, but not flowers.

Look on the underside of a fern leaf (or frond). The brown spots contain spores.

Parts of a plant

Flower

Bud

Leaf

Fruit

Stem

Roots

Parts of a flower

Petal

Pistil (female)
- Stigma
- Style
- Ovule
- Ovary

Anther

Filament

Stamen (male)

Sepal

Receptacle

Lawns are often cut too short for you to see this, but even grass produces tiny flowers!

TRY THIS...

MAKE A SEED BOMB

Help nature by playing the part of a seed-spreader!

- You will need to buy a packet of mixed flower seeds.

- Empty the seeds into a bucket. Mix in 2 handfuls of **compost**.

- In a cup, mix 1 tablespoon of flour with water until it is runny, like glue.

- Add this to the seeds and mix until you can roll it into a ball.

- Leave the ball to dry overnight, and then throw it onto a bare patch of garden. If there is no rain, use water from a water butt.

- Over time, the seeds should grow into plants.

Making more

Gardeners grow new plants from seeds, but also from other parts of the plant. This is called **propagation**. New plants can grow from tiny shoots called cuttings, or by dividing a clump into two sections and planting them apart.

FRUIT TREES

Certain types of plant protect their seeds inside fruit. These fruits are not always edible, but some of them are sweet or juicy, such as apples and berries. Some are hard, like walnuts and hazelnuts. Avocados, green beans, pumpkins and cucumbers are also fruits, because they have seeds on the inside.

Cherry trees have beautiful blossoms in the spring.

Half of the world's apples are grown in China.

Plums grow on small trees that can fit into most gardens.

Watermelons grow on the ground.

Lemons need sunshine and protection from frost in the winter.

It's easy to grow strawberries in a pot on a sunny patio.

Almonds grow on trees, just like apples do!

Which fruit?

Fruit that grows on trees, including apples, peaches, plums, pears and cherries, are called **top fruit**. **Soft fruit** grows on shorter plants such as vines, bushes or canes. These include grapes, blackcurrants and all kinds of berries.

Protecting plants

A clever gardener will plant fruit trees in the best position for them to produce a bumper crop. Fruit trees need sun for the fruit to ripen, and shelter from the wind and rain. They are often planted along a south-facing wall or fence. The soil needs to be well drained (not soggy), with compost or manure mixed around the tree roots.

Pests such as caterpillars, aphids (pictured), beetles and moths may attack fruit trees.

Ripening fruit

Fruit not only protects seeds, it also helps attract creatures that will eat the seeds and spread them far and wide in their droppings. Ripe fruit is the most appealing, as more of the starch inside it has turned to sugar, and so the fruit is softer and sweeter. Spreading the seeds helps to ensure the plant's survival, as there is less competition for light and space.

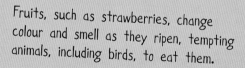

Fruits, such as strawberries, change colour and smell as they ripen, tempting animals, including birds, to eat them.

TRY THIS...

MAKE YOUR FRUIT RIPEN!

Bananas release a gas called ethene that has a transforming effect on other fruit:

- Find a fruit that is not yet ripe enough to eat. Pears, peaches, kiwis and tomatoes work well.

- Place the fruit in a paper bag with a ripe banana. Fold over the top and leave it overnight.

- Check the fruit, and if it still appears unripe, reseal the bag and leave for one more day.

- The ethene gas speeds up the ripening process. Your green or crunchy fruit should soon be edible.

GROW YOUR OWN

Vegetables are plants, such as potatoes, broccoli and peas, that we eat as food. Growing your own vegetables is rewarding, but you need to be prepared to look after your plants. Your vegetable plot could be as big as an allotment or as small as a plant pot.

Beans make the soil more fertile, which makes corn grow much better. They can also be planted next to tomatoes.

Cabbages and onions grow well side by side.

Good for growth

Clever planting of different vegetables can help to keep pests away and even improve the flavour of the foods. Some plants benefit by being close to each other, while others should be grown at a distance. This is called **companion planting**. Different plants take different nutrients from the soil, so it is wise to move them from year to year. This is known as **crop rotation**.

A border of marigolds stops animals raiding the veg patch, and gives off a scent that keeps insects away.

Vegetables can be planted with members of the same family. Chillis and peppers are in the potato family, as are aubergines. Celery and parsnips are related to carrots, while lettuce is related to sunflowers, artichokes and dandelions.

The carrots we eat today are orange, but originally wild carrots were purple and yellow.

Broccoli and carrots grow well together, but should be kept away from peppers and tomatoes.

Strong-smelling garlic keeps aphids away from tomatoes, but is not a good neighbour for peas.

Through the ages

Prehistoric people did not plant and grow their own vegetables. They found them growing in the wild. These foods were the ancestors of modern vegetables, and looked very different. Many modern varieties have been **selectively bred** to grow bigger or be less vulnerable to disease and bad weather.

Brilliant benefits

Home-grown vegetables are often cheaper than ones bought from a shop. You can also produce them naturally without the use of chemicals.

GARDEN HERBS

If you like eating pasta, you might be surprised to know that you can 'grow' your own pasta sauce quite easily. All you need is some pots to grow cherry tomatoes and a **herb** called basil, and a sunny spot.

How to grow herbs

Herbs are easy to grow and maintain. They have a lovely aroma, and almost all herbs are edible and tasty! You can grow herbs in a container on the patio, a sunny windowsill or in a flower bed in the garden.

PARSLEY

CHIVES

THYME

BASIL

FRESH HERBY PIZZA

Put your homegrown herbs to good use with this yummy recipe!

- Spray olive oil on a fresh pizza base, then sprinkle salt and pepper to taste.

- Chop some mozzarella cheese and sprinkle over the pizza base.

- Cover with cherry tomatoes, some fresh basil leaves and a few small thyme leaves. Sprinkle some parmesan cheese on top.

- With an adult's help, bake your pizza at 180°C for 10-12 minutes, until the cheese is golden and crusty.

BE CAREFUL

Ask an adult for help with using a knife or an oven.

Herbs like rosemary, oregano, sage, thyme, marjoram and lavender can be planted close together. They need lots of sun and a little water.

Oregano contains chemicals that can repel insects.

ROSEMARY

SAGE

OREGANO

GARDEN CREATURES

You may get many visitors to a garden – not all of them human. It can be a home or a feeding place for insects and other minibeasts, birds, wild mammals and neighbourhood cats.

Hedgehog
These prickly creatures make a nest in leaf litter and **hibernate** through the coldest winter months. When they're awake, they eat garden pests such as slugs and snails.

Caterpillar
These creatures are the young, or larvae, of butterflies and moths. As adults, moths and butterflies are important for pollination, but as caterpillars, they munch through leaves.

DID YOU KNOW?
Ladybirds produce nasty smelling, toxic, yellow 'blood' if threatened by predators.

Fox
Foxes are **nocturnal**, and feed on bugs, worms, small mammals and fallen fruit. You may hear foxes in January when they howl to find a mate.

Ladybird
Easily identified by their spotted wing cases, gardeners welcome these bright beetles as they gobble up aphids that cause damage to plants.

Earthworm

These creatures are really important. They tunnel through the soil, allowing air and water to circulate through it. They also break down dead matter, adding nutrients to the soil.

Slugs and snails

You might see the slimy trail left behind by these molluscs, or the holes left after they have feasted on plants. Both move around using a muscular foot, and rest in damp, dark places.

Slug

Snail

Wasp

Bees and wasps

These striped insects, and the hoverflies that mimic them, are responsible for pollinating a huge number of flowering plants, including many of those we grow for fruit and vegetables.

Bee

Squirrel

A squirrel can be seen running along a fence or jumping between branches. They can damage plants by eating their buds, fruit and bulbs, or by burying nuts in the lawn before winter.

Frog

DID YOU KNOW?

A single frog can eat 100 bugs in one night!

Frogs and toads

Both of these amphibians may visit your garden if there is a pond or lake nearby. They hibernate in winter.

Spider

These eight-legged minibeasts are a gardener's friend, as they prey on many pests. Look for a web glistening in the morning dew or frost.

Toad

GARDEN BIRDS

All sorts of birds make their homes in a garden. Make yours a bird-friendly space. Use nuts and seeds to tempt them to visit. Try to observe which birds prefer which foods. Leave water out for them to drink. Are there any birds that come back again and again?

Male

Female

Chaffinch

Chaffinches are stout birds with double white stripes on their wings. The males have a pink breast and bluish crown. Females are greenish–brown.

European goldfinch

American goldfinch

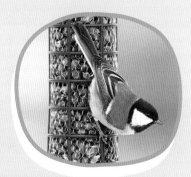

Goldfinch

Beautiful, bright feathers make this small bird easy to spot. They love to eat sunflower seeds; put them in a garden feeder or, if you have the space, grow some sunflowers.

Great tit

The great tit has a black cap and throat, with white cheeks. They move in groups, but aren't friendly to other birds. Common in Europe and Asia, great tits will happily make use of garden nesting boxes.

American robin

European robin

Robin

Easy to spot with their famous red chest, robins are active all year round. They eat insects and worms, pouncing on them and plucking them from the lawn or flower beds.

Wren

The tiny wren has a long, thin beak and a striped belly. Look for the pale face stripe, like an eyebrow. It flies close to the ground, and can be spotted in the bushes or hedges.

Magpie

Magpies seem to be black and white, but in flight you can see the glossy blue, purple and green on their wings and tail. They are intelligent birds that prey on the eggs and babies of other birds.

Starling

Starlings are noisy birds that fly in large flocks. Their white specks disappear in winter, leaving shiny green and blue feathers. Starlings can copy many sounds including phones and car alarms!

Male

Female

House sparrow

House sparrows are friendly birds and are very common in gardens everywhere. Their feathers are mostly brown, but the male has a black bib on its chest.

Blackbird

You cannot miss this regular visitor to the garden, with its bright yellow eye ring and beak. Females have duller brown feathers. When they are not singing from the rooftops, blackbirds are busy looking for worms in the grass.

TRY THIS...

MAKE A BIRD HOUSE

Use an empty milk or juice carton to make a weather-proof nesting box. Ask an adult to help with the tricky bits.

- Cover the plastic pouring spout with tape to close it.

- Cut out a circle 5 cm wide, enough for a small bird to fit through.

- For a perch, make a small hole 5 cm below the circle, and insert a twig or stick.

- Punch a small hole in the top tab to tie a piece of string.

- Decorate however you like.

- Hang your bird house from a fence or a tree, and wait for the birds to discover it.

A GARDEN ECOSYSTEM

The plants in a garden depend on the creatures that visit it and vice versa. They make up an ecosystem, where all the living things in one area are important to each other's survival. A garden food chain shows what is eaten, or consumed, by what, and joins together to form a food web.

Plants

Insects

Making food

A food chain is made up of three groups. The first is the **producers**: all the plants in a garden. They are called this because they produce their own food using **photosynthesis**. Photosynthesis is the process where plants use sunlight to turn carbon dioxide (from the air) and water into food. Oxygen is released as a by-product.

Eat and be eaten

Next in the food chain are the **consumers**. Plant-eaters (called **herbivores**) are primary consumers. These include many insects, and birds such as sparrows and finches that eat seeds. Secondary consumers are meat-eaters (**insectivores**, **carnivores** or **omnivores**) such as robins, blackbirds, hedgehogs, bats and foxes.

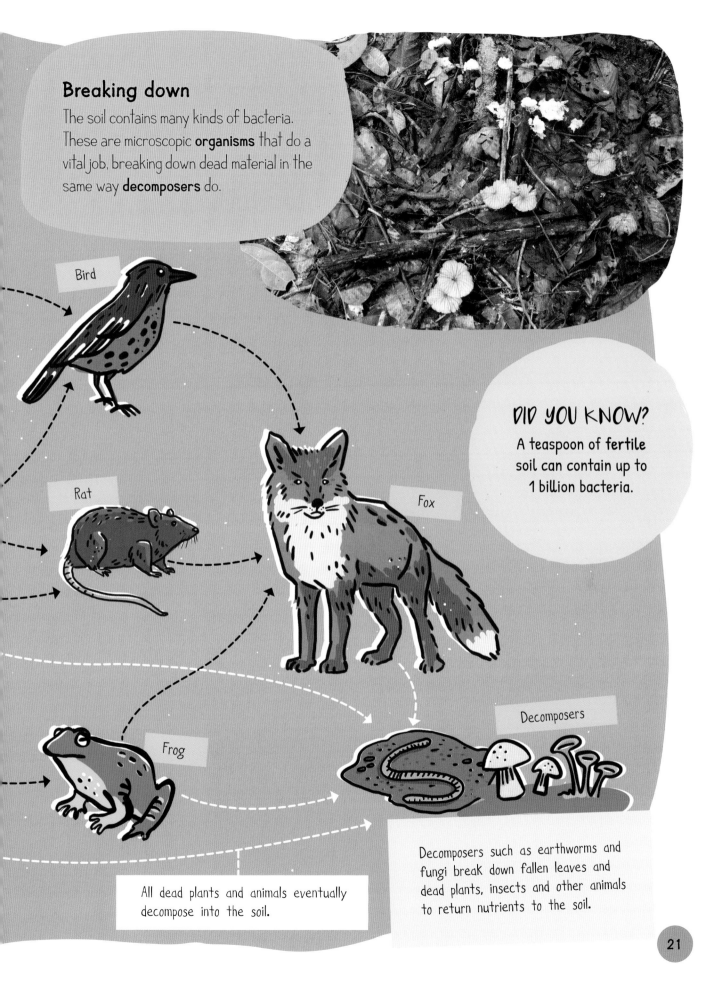

Breaking down

The soil contains many kinds of bacteria. These are microscopic **organisms** that do a vital job, breaking down dead material in the same way **decomposers** do.

Bird

Rat

Fox

Frog

Decomposers

DID YOU KNOW?
A teaspoon of **fertile** soil can contain up to 1 billion bacteria.

All dead plants and animals eventually decompose into the soil.

Decomposers such as earthworms and fungi break down fallen leaves and dead plants, insects and other animals to return nutrients to the soil.

THROUGH THE SEASONS

During a year in the life of a garden, things grow, change and die, sometimes several times a year. There are different jobs to do in every season.

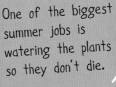

One of the biggest summer jobs is watering the plants so they don't die.

Summer

Trees are covered in leaves. Gardens are full of colourful flowers, which attract butterflies and bees. The sunshine encourages weeds to grow – dig them out before they take over!

Spring

Fruit trees blossom in the spring, while other trees sprout buds before their green leaves appear. Many flowers that grow from bulbs, such as crocuses, daffodils, tulips and snowdrops, will appear. As the days get warmer, grass grows again and you will hear the birds singing to attract a mate. Look for frogspawn in ponds, and bumblebees flying through the air.

Spring is the time to plant seeds in pots. Keep them in a greenhouse or on a windowsill.

22

Autumn

As leaves on the trees change colour and begin to fall off, lots of berries and fruits ripen. That brings squirrels, gathering food for the colder months. Clear the dead leaves and add them to the compost heap (see page 27). You can prepare for spring by planting bulbs and sowing grass seed on the lawn.

GARDEN JOBS

There's a tool for every gardening job. Can you help with raking leaves or digging a hole for a plant?

TROWEL for digging the soil

RAKE for collecting fallen leaves

SECATEURS for pruning bushes

SHEARS for cutting branches

DID YOU KNOW?

Hedgehogs, toads and all kinds of bugs such as millipedes, worms, caterpillars and woodlice make their homes in piles of dead leaves. Before you rake them up, or have fun with the leaf blower, check underneath them first.

Winter

Move pots and containers into sheltered places, and cover up the most vulnerable plants to protect them from the frost. This is a good time for bird watching, when there are few leaves on the trees, and new species have **migrated** for the coldest months.

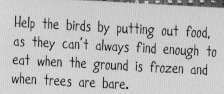

Help the birds by putting out food, as they can't always find enough to eat when the ground is frozen and when trees are bare.

GARDEN HELPERS

Pollinators help plants, and plants help pollinators. It's a two-way relationship where everyone's a winner. There are some things you can do to make your garden more attractive so the pollinators come calling.

DID YOU KNOW?

Bees and butterflies are the most widely known pollinators, but wasps, hoverflies, moths, flies, mosquitoes, beetles, birds and bats also carry pollen between flowers.

Flower friends

Bees visit flowers for two reasons: to suck up nectar and to collect pollen, which they feed to their young (larvae). In return, the pollen is transferred from flower to flower, fertilising them so they can reproduce (see pages 8–9). Other creatures collect pollen by brushing against it when they visit plants to find nectar, fruit, nuts or just to rest for a while.

How pollination works

1. A bee crawls into the flower to collect nectar and pollen.

2. Pollen from stamens sticks to the bee's body and legs.

3. The bee flies to the next flower. Some of the pollen brushes off onto the pistils.

MAKE A WILDFLOWER SEED MAT

Do your prep work indoors, and you can plant wildflowers whatever the weather.

- Spread out a damp **biodegradable** kitchen cloth in the kitchen.

- Place two pieces of kitchen towel, side by side, on the cloth.

- Sprinkle a packet of wildflower seeds across the paper, as evenly as you can. Cover with two more pieces of kitchen towel and press down with your hands.

- Place the now-damp kitchen towel carefully onto a patch of bare soil, and cover with about 0.5 cm of fine compost. Watch and wait for the wildflowers to appear! Water them if they get too dry.

Why pollinators matter

Without these creatures, farmers could not produce the amount of food needed to feed the human population. One out of every three mouthfuls of what we eat depends on pollination taking place. Scientists are worried that important bee, butterfly and moth species are dying out due to the use of chemical fertilisers, diseases and loss of habitat. People and wildlife will suffer if pollinators drop in number.

Bee-friendly

You can make a garden more attractive to bees and other insects by:

- Choosing flowers of different shapes and colours. Butterflies and bees are especially attracted to blue or purple flowers

- Planting dahlias, lavender and sunflowers

- Avoiding the use of pesticides

- Using wildflowers or flowers grown from seed instead of those bought from shops

COMPOSTING

Composting is a clever way of helping the environment. **Microorganisms** and minibeasts turn kitchen and garden waste into precious food for your garden.

DID YOU KNOW?
Composting for just one year can save global warming gases equivalent to all the carbon dioxide that your family washing machine makes in three months.

Pile it high!

Compost plays a very important role by ensuring that the soil doesn't pile up with waste. The composted waste feeds plants that grow from the ground, and they in turn feed animals. It's all part of a natural cycle. When you create a compost pile in your garden, you also help to reduce the amount of stuff that ends up in bins and is sent to the landfills.

Compost is called 'black gold' by gardeners, because it provides essential nutrients for plant growth, and also improves soil structure.

TRY THIS...

COMPOST IN A BOTTLE

Try this 'rotten' experiment and become an expert composter!

- Clean a plastic bottle and layer it with soil, food scraps, leaves and some garden fertiliser. Spray a little water on each layer, but do not soak!

- Tape the bottle shut and keep it in a dark cupboard.

- Check the bottle after 6 months to see if you've got some lovely homemade compost!

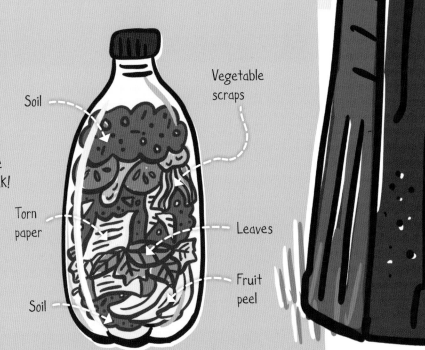

Soil

Vegetable scraps

Torn paper

Leaves

Fruit peel

Soil

What can you put into compost?

The best compost is a mixture of green things, such as fruit and vegetable peelings, teabags and grass cuttings, along with brown things, such as cardboard, egg boxes and paper. Simply put, waste + moisture + warmth + air + microorganisms + time = compost. DO NOT add cooked food to your compost as it will attract pests, such as rats.

Sustainable gardening

Some good habits can help your garden become **sustainable**. This means it can flourish naturally without needing chemicals (like pesticides or weedkillers) or too much water. Composting is part of sustainable gardening.

Reuse and recycle

Compost isn't the only thing you can reuse in your garden. Water is precious, so collect rainwater in a water butt and use it in your watering can instead of filling it from the tap. You can also gather seeds from your plants, and save them in a cool, dry, dark place ready to sow in new places the following year.

GREEN SPACES

You don't need a garden to be able to grow things. Be inventive with containers and hanging baskets, or find any available space such as a window box or balcony.

You can even grow a vertical 'green' wall with indoor plants.

Hang extra containers from fences, or fix them to walls.

Cover drains with tubs of flowers.

Feed me!

Fruit and vegetables will grow in tiny spaces, but they will quickly use the nutrients in the soil. As well as keeping them watered, you should feed them regularly with special plant food. Strawberries and cherry tomatoes grow well in hanging baskets, and you can grow potatoes in a sack!

Indoor gardening

Your home will benefit from having plants inside, too. As well as brightening a room, they help to clean and filter the air. Spider plants and peace lilies improve the air quality, while aloe vera is easy to care for, and its juicy insides can be used to soothe cuts and burns.

Plant salad leaves and herbs in a container on your window sill.

Plants can grow almost anywhere!

WHAT CAN YOU DO?

There are many ways you can create a 'healthy' garden.

- Spreading mulch (like shredded bark or grass clippings) on the ground reduces the growth of weeds.

- Don't plant the same plants in the same spots year after year. This keeps away the pests that attack specific plants.

- Plant wildflowers that encourage pollinators such as bees and butterflies to visit.

QUIZ

1. When do fruit trees blossom?

a) Spring

b) Summer

c) All year

2. Which is a female part of a flower?

a) Anther

b) Filament

c) Stigma

3. Where do alpine plants grow best?

a) A rockery

b) A pond

c) A shady corner

4. Which gas makes fruit ripen?

a) Polythene

b) Ethene

c) Benzene

5. What is the process of growing new plants from other parts of the same plant called?

a) Irrigating

b) Propagating

c) Conjugating

6. Which plants last for the longest time?

a) Annuals

b) Biennials

c) Perennials

7. What do ferns and mosses produce instead of flowers and seeds?

a) Spuds

b) Spades

c) Spores

8. Which of these is NOT a decomposer in the food chain?

a) Dead plants

b) Bacteria

c) Fungus

ANSWERS: 1a, 2c, 3a, 4b, 5b, 6c, 7c, 8a.

GLOSSARY

annual a plant that grows and dies within one year

bacteria tiny, single-celled organisms

biennial a plant with a two-year growing cycle

biodegradable able to be broken down naturally by living organisms

carnivore a creature that eats meat

companion planting close planting so plants protect each other from pests

compost decayed organic material used to fertilise plants

consumer in a food chain, a creature that eats plants or other creatures

crop rotation changing the type of plants grown in one spot to improve the soil

deciduous a plant that loses its leaves in winter

decomposer an organism that breaks down organic material

evergreen a plant that keeps its leaves throughout the year

fertile good for growing things in

fertilise to enable a living thing to reproduce

herb a plant used for flavouring, perfume or medicine

herbivore a creature that eats only plant-based food

insectivore a creature that eats mostly insects

microorganism an organism that is too tiny to see without a microscope (for example, a bacterium, virus or fungus)

migration seasonal movement from one location to another

nectar a sugary liquid made by flowers

nocturnal active during the night

nutrients substances that help growth and healthy living

omnivore a creature that eats plants and creatures

organic matter coming from living things

organism a living thing, such as bacteria, plants or animals

perennial a plant that lives for more than two years

photosynthesis the way green plants produce food

pollinator a creature that transfers pollen from flower to flower

predator an animal that eats other animals

producer the first part of a food chain, consisting of plants and algae

propagating growing new plants from plant parts, such as cuttings

rock garden, rockery a garden made of piles of rocks with soil between them

selective breeding breeding specially chosen plants to get desired characteristics, such as sweeter fruit or larger flowers

shrub a low-growing woody plant

soft fruit small fruit that grows on bushes or vines

spore the reproductive part of some plants

sustainable keeping the balance of nature (by using natural methods of growing)

top fruit fruit that grows on trees

INDEX

FURTHER READING

These websites and books will give you lots more ideas about the great outdoors!

www.wildlifetrusts.org/gardening

www.wildlifewatch.org.uk/explore-wildlife/habitats/towns-and-gardens

www.discoverwildlife.com/how-to/wildlife-gardening

www.rspb.org.uk/fun-and-learning/for-kids/facts-about-nature/facts-about-habitats/urban-and-suburban

www.nationaltrust.org.uk/children-and-nature

Garden Flowers (The Great Nature Hunt)
Cath Senker (Franklin Watts, 2019)

Planting and Growing (Outdoor Explorers)
Sandy Green (Franklin Watts, 2013)

British Trees and Flowers (Nature in Your Neighbourhood)
Clare Collinson (Franklin Watts, 2018)

Plants (Moving up with Science)
Peter Riley (Franklin Watts, 2016)